Documenting Sources in MLA Style: 2021 Update

A Bedford/St. Martin's Supplement

bedford/st.martin's
Macmillan Learning
Boston | New York

Manufactured in the United States of America.

1 2 3 4 5 6   26 25 24 23 22 21

For information, write: Bedford/St. Martin's, 75 Arlington Street, Boston, MA 02116

ISBN 978-1-319-43743-5

Contents

Contents

In English courses and in some humanities courses, you may be asked to use the MLA (Modern Language Association) system for documenting sources. The guidelines in this booklet follow those set forth in the *MLA Handbook*, 9th edition (2021).

Rather than thinking of these guidelines simply as rules to be followed, try seeing them as guidelines for participating in an academic community—a community in which the exchange and extension of ideas requires a system. Even though this booklet presents a system for citing many different kinds of sources, it doesn't cover everything; at times you may have to think critically to adapt the guidelines to the source you are using.

Elements of MLA citations

MLA documentation consists of in-text citations that refer to a list of works cited at the end of a project. There are often several possible ways to cite a source in the list of works cited. Think carefully about your context for using the source so you can identify the pieces of information that you should include and any other information that might be helpful to your readers. The first step is to identify elements that are commonly found in works that writers cite.

Author and title

The first two elements, both of which are needed for most sources, are the author's name and the title of the work. Each of these elements is followed by a period.

Author.
Title.

Container

The next step is to identify elements of what MLA calls the "container" for the work—any larger work that contains the source you are citing. The context in which you are discussing the source and the context in which you find the source will help you determine what counts as a container in each case. Some works are self-contained; if you watch a movie in a theater, the movie title is the title of your source, and you won't identify a separate container title. But if you watch the same movie on a streaming service, the container title is the name of the website or application on which you watched the movie. Thinking about sources as nested in larger containers may help you visualize how a citation works. (Also see the diagram below.)

The elements you may include in the "container" part of your citation include, in order, the title of the container; the names of contributors such as editors or translators; the version or edition; the volume and issue numbers or other numbers such as season and episode; the publisher; the date of publication; and a location such as the page number(s), DOI, permalink, or URL. These elements are separated by commas, and the end of the container is marked with a period.

Most sources will not include *all* these pieces of information, so include only the elements that are relevant and available for the source that you are citing. If your container is itself a part of some larger container, such as a database, simply add information about the second container after the first one. You will find many examples of how elements and containers are combined to create works cited entries on pages 10–30 of this booklet. The guidelines box on pages 12–14 also provides details about the information required for each element.

BASIC CONTAINER INFORMATION

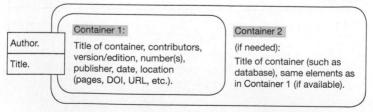

WORKS CITED ENTRY (ONE CONTAINER)

author   title   title of container (edited book)

Smith, Zadie. "Speaking in Tongues." *The Glorious American Essay: One Hundred*

                                        contributor   publisher

Essays from Colonial Times to the Present, edited by Phillip Lopate, Pantheon,

            location

year   (pages)

2020, pp. 886–900.

WORKS CITED ENTRY (TWO CONTAINERS)

author   title

Carey, Craig. "Realism and Recording: Remixing Literary and Media History."

        title of
   container 1 (journal)   volume, issue   date   pages

American Literary Realism, vol. 53, no. 3, spring 2021, pp. 198–203.

    title of
   container 2
   (database)   location (DOI)

JSTOR, https://doi.org/10.5406/amerlitereal.53.3.0198.

MLA in-text citations

MLA style requires you to supply an in-text citation each time you quote, paraphrase, summarize, or otherwise integrate material from a source. In-text citations are made with a combination of signal phrases and parenthetical references and provide the information your readers need to locate the full citations in the list of works cited at the end of the text.

A signal phrase introduces information taken from a source; usually the signal phrase includes the author's name — either a first and last name if the source is being mentioned for the first time in the essay or just a last name for later citations. Parenthetical citations include at least a page number (except for unpaginated sources, such as those found online) or sometimes another locator, such as a time stamp. The list of works cited provides publication information about the source. There is a direct connection between the signal phrase or parenthetical citation and the first word or words in the works cited entry.

SAMPLE CITATION USING A SIGNAL PHRASE

In a time when literature and higher education were seen as privileges, Robert Zaretsky notes that Simone Weil considered literature education "a tool for revolution" (17).

SAMPLE PARENTHETICAL CITATION

In a time when literature and higher education were seen as privileges, Simone Weil considered literature education "a tool for revolution" (Zaretsky 17).

WORKS CITED ENTRY

Zaretsky, Robert. *The Subversive Simone Weil: A Life in Five Ideas*. U of Chicago P, 2021.

Directory to MLA in-text citation models

1. Author named in a signal phrase, 5
2. Author named in a parenthetical citation, 5
3. Digital or nonprint source, 5
4. Two authors, 5
5. Three or more authors, 6
6. Organization as author, 6
7. Unknown author, 6
8. Two or more works by the same author, 6
9. Two or more authors with the same last name, 7
10. Indirect source (source quoted in another source), 7
11. Multivolume work, 7
12. Work in an anthology or a collection, 7
13. Government source, 8
14. Entire work, 8
15. Two or more sources in one citation, 8
16. Repeated citations from the same source, 8
17. Personal communication or social media source, 9
18. Literary work (novel, play, poem), 9
19. Sacred text, 9
20. Encyclopedia or dictionary entry, 10
21. Visual, 10
22. Legal source, 10

1. Author named in a signal phrase   Ordinarily, introduce the material being cited with a signal phrase that includes the author's name. Give the author's full name in the first mention and only the last name in later signal phrases.

Stan Lee claims that his comic-book character Thor was actually "the first regularly published superhero to speak in a consistently archaic manner" (199).

2. Author named in a parenthetical citation   When you do not mention the author in a signal phrase, include the author's last name before the page number(s), if any, in parentheses. Do not use punctuation between the author's name and the page number(s).

The word *Bollywood* can be insulting because it implies that Indian movies are merely "a derivative of the American film industry" (Chopra 9).

3. Digital or nonprint source   Give enough information in a signal phrase or in parentheses for readers to locate the source in your list of works cited—at least the author's name or the source's title. If the source lacks page numbers but has numbered paragraphs, sections, or divisions, use those numbers with the appropriate abbreviation in your parenthetical citation. Do not add such numbers if the source itself does not use them.

As a *Slate* analysis notes, "Prominent sports psychologists get praised for their successes and don't get grief for their failures" (Engber).

The author's son points out that his father and Ralph Waldo Emerson, in their lives and their writing, "together . . . met the needs of nearly all that is worthy in human nature" (Hawthorne, ch. 4).

When quoting, paraphrasing, or summarizing from an audio or a video source, include a time stamp for the material you are citing.

Kalika Bali explains that as the "digital divide between languages" with and without technological resources grows, "the divide between the communities that speak these languages is expanding" (00:04:40–51).

4. Two authors   Name both authors in a signal phrase or in parentheses.

Sandra Gilbert and Susan Gubar point out that in the Grimm version of "Snow White," the king "never actually appears in this story at all" (37).

5. Three or more authors   In a signal phrase, use the first author's name followed by a phrase such as *and others*, or list all the authors' names. In parentheses, use the first author's name followed by *et al.* ("and others").

> Similarly, as Belenky and colleagues assert, examining the lives of women expands our understanding of human development (7).

> Similarly, a "misreading of women" is the unfortunate result of defining human development by men's intellectual development (Belenky et al. 7).

6. Organization as author   Give the group's full name in a signal phrase; in parentheses, shorten the name to the first noun and any preceding adjectives, removing any articles (*A, An, The*).

> According to a survey by the Girl Scouts of the United States of America, seventy-five percent of young people want to elect more women to Congress.

> One survey reports that seventy-five percent of young people want to elect more women to Congress (Girl Scouts).

7. Unknown author   Use the full title of the source if it is brief. If the title is more than a few words, shorten it to the first noun and any preceding adjectives (not including *A, An*, or *The*) in parentheses. Place the title in quotation marks or italics according to the style used in the list of works cited.

> Coca-Cola and other similarly well-known companies often avoid public politics to uphold their images as "emblems of American harmony" ("CEO Activism").

8. Two or more works by the same author   Mention the title of the work in a signal phrase, or include a short version of the title in parentheses.

> In "The Intoxicated," Jackson illustrates how older generations are often afraid of the change brought about by young people with her protagonist's uneasy reaction to the girl's comments, fretting "that when he was young people had not talked like that" (7).

> Old Man Warner complains that the younger people calling for change will next "be wanting to go back to living in caves" (Jackson, "Lottery" 295).

9. Two or more authors with the same last name Include the author's first and last name in a signal phrase or their first initial and last name in parentheses.

> One approach to the problem is to introduce nutrition literacy at the elementary level in public schools (E. Chen 15).

10. Indirect source (source quoted in another source) Use the abbreviation *qtd. in* to indicate that you are using a source that is cited in another source.

> Jordan "silently marveled" at her Black students' dismissal of Black language in the novel (qtd. in Baker-Bell 24).

11. Multivolume work If you cite more than one volume of a multivolume work in your text, note the volume number and then the page number(s), with a colon and one space between them, in your parenthetical citation.

> Modernist writers prized experimentation and gradually even sought to blur the line between poetry and prose, according to Forster (3: 150).

If you cite only one volume of the work in your text, do not include the volume number in the citation.

12. Work in an anthology or a collection Use the name of the author of the work, not the editor of the anthology. Use the page number(s) from the anthology.

> In "How to Write Iranian-America, or the Last Essay," Porochista Khakpour details degrading experiences with English language instructors "who look to you with the shine of love but the stench of pity" (3).

In the list of works cited, the work is alphabetized under Khakpour, the author of the essay, not under the names of the editors of the anthology.

Khakpour, Porochista. "How to Write Iranian-America, or the Last Essay." *The Good Immigrant: 26 Writers Reflect on America*, edited by Nikesh Shukla and Chimene Suleyman, Little, Brown, 2019, pp. 3–15.

13. Government source   In a signal phrase, include the name of the agency or governing body as given in the works cited list. In a parenthetical citation, shorten the name.

> The National Endowment for the Arts notes that social media and online events play a significant role in "showcasing the importance of the arts to the vitality of the nation" (15).

> Social media and online events play a significant role in "showcasing the importance of the arts to the vitality of the nation" (National Endowment 15).

If you cite more than one agency or department from the same government in your essay, you may choose to standardize the names by beginning with the name of the government (see item 57 in the works cited list section). In that case, when shortening the names, give enough of each one to differentiate the authors: *(United States, National Endowment); (United States, Environmental Protection)*.

14. Entire work   Use the author's name in a signal phrase or a parenthetical citation.

> Michael Pollan explores the issues surrounding food production and consumption from a political angle.

15. Two or more sources in one citation   List the authors (or titles) in alphabetical order and separate them with semicolons.

> Economists recommend that employment be redefined to include unpaid domestic labor (Clark 148; Nevins 39).

16. Repeated citations from the same source   If you cite a source more than once in a paragraph, you may omit the author's name after the first mention in the paragraph as long as it is clear that you are still referring to the same source.

> Family expectations are at the heart of *Everything I Never Told You*, a debut novel in which a daughter shrinks from a mother who forces her to read books on science and medicine "to inspire her, to show her what she could accomplish" (Ng 73). But teenage Lydia commits herself to standing up to her overbearing mother, promising that "she will tell her mother: enough" (274).

17. Personal communication or social media source   Use the name of the author as given in the works cited list.

> Grammar Girl explains that "Irish English uses many words differently from American and British English, and 'myself' is just one example."

18. Literary work (novel, play, poem)   Because literary works are often available in many different editions, cite the page number(s) from the edition you used followed by a semicolon; then give other identifying information that will lead readers to the passage in any edition. For a novel, indicate the part and/or chapter: *(175; ch. 4)*.

> In utter despair, Dostoyevsky's character Mitya wonders aloud about the "terrible tragedies realism inflicts on people" (376; bk. 8, ch. 2).

For a play, indicate the page number, then the act and/or scene: *(37; sc. 1)*. For a verse play, give only the act, scene, and line numbers, separated by periods.

> Marullus expresses his anger at the commoners' celebrations, shouting, "You blocks, you stones, you worse than senseless things!" (Shakespeare 1.1.40).

For a poem, cite the part (if there is one) and line(s), separated by a period.

> Whitman speculates, "All goes onward and outward, nothing collapses, / And to die is different from what anyone supposed, and luckier" (6.129–30).

If you are citing only line numbers, use the word *line(s)* in the first citation (*lines 21–22*) and the line number(s) alone in subsequent citations (*34–36*).

19. Sacred text   The first time you cite the work, give the title of the work as in the works cited entry, followed by the book, chapter, and verse (or their equivalent), separated with periods. Common abbreviations for books of the Bible are acceptable in a parenthetical citation. Omit the source's title from the parentheses in all citations after the first.

> He ignored the familiar warning: "Pride goes before destruction, and a haughty spirit before a fall" (*New Oxford Annotated Bible*, Prov. 16.18).

20. Encyclopedia or dictionary entry   For reference work entries without a named author, give the title of the entry in quotation marks.

The word *crocodile* has a complex etymology ("Crocodile" 139–40).

21. Visual   If you cite information from a numbered visual in a source and do not present the visual in your essay, use the abbreviation "fig." and the original figure number in place of a page number in your parenthetical citation: *(Manning, fig. 4)*. If you refer to the figure in your text, spell out the word *figure*. If the visual does not have a figure number in the source, use the visual's title or a description in your text and cite the author and page number as for any other source. If you are citing a work of art or other stand-alone visual, follow the advice in item 3.

For visuals that you use in your essay, include a figure or table number and a caption with information about the source (see pp. 31–32).

22. Legal source   For a legislative act (law) or court case, name the act or case either in a signal phrase or in parentheses. Italicize the names of cases but not the names of acts.

The Jones Act of 1917 granted US citizenship to Puerto Ricans.

Dred Scott v. Sandford, which concluded that neither free nor enslaved Black people could be citizens of the United States, may have been the US Supreme Court's worst decision.

MLA list of works cited

An alphabetized list of works cited, which appears at the end of your project, gives publication information for each source you have cited. (For more information about preparing the list, see pp. 32–33; for a sample list of works cited, see p. 40.)

Directory to MLA works cited models

General guidelines for the works cited list

In the list of works cited, include only sources that you have quoted, summarized, or paraphrased in your project. MLA's guidelines apply to a wide variety of sources. At times, however, you may find that you have to adapt the guidelines and models in this section to source types you encounter in your research.

Elements of a works cited list entry

A works cited entry typically includes the following elements, or pieces of information:

- The author (if a work has one)
- The title of the source
- The title of the larger work in which the source is located (MLA calls this a "container") — a collection, a journal, a website, a database, and so on
- As much of the following information as is available about the source and the container, listed in this order:
  - Contributor (such as editor, translator, director, performer)
  - Version
  - Volume and issue numbers (or other similar numbers)
  - Publisher or sponsor
  - Publication date
  - Location of the source (such as page numbers, DOI, URL, time stamp)

Not all sources will require every element. For more information on identifying and organizing source elements, see page 2. See specific models in this section for more details.

Authors

- Arrange the list of works cited alphabetically either by authors' last names or by titles for works with no authors.
- For the first author, place the last name first, a comma, and the first name and any initials. Give a second author's name as first name followed by last name; separate two authors' names with *and*. For three or more authors, use *et al*. after the first author's name.

General guidelines for the works cited list (*cont.*)

Authors

- Spell out *editor, translator, director*, and so on.
- For organization authors, list the name as it appears in the source. If the name begins with an article (*A, An*, or *The*), omit it.

Titles

- In titles of works, capitalize all words except articles (*a, an, the*), prepositions (such as *of, with*), coordinating conjunctions (such as *and*), and the *to* in infinitives (*How to Run a Marathon*) — unless the word is first or last in the title or subtitle.
- Use quotation marks for titles of articles and other short works.
- Italicize titles of books and other long works, including websites.

Publication information

- Use the complete version of publishers' names, except for terms such as *Inc.* and *Co.*; if the name begins with an article (*A, An*, or *The*), omit it. Retain terms such as *Books* and *Publishers*.
- For a publisher with *University* and *Press* in its name, use *U* and *P* for each word. (Do not abbreviate or omit *Press* if *University* is not also in the publisher's name.)
- For a book, take the name of the publisher from the title page (or from the copyright page if it is not on the title page). For a website, the publisher might be at the bottom of a page or on the *About* page. If a work has two or more publishers, separate the names with a forward slash.
- If the title of a website and the publisher's name are the same or similar, use the title of the site and omit the publisher.

Dates

- For a book, give the most recent year on the title page or the copyright page.
- For an article from a periodical such as a newspaper or a journal, use the most specific date given, whether it is a month and year, a full date, or a season (*spring 2021*).
- For a web source, use the posting date, the copyright date, or the most recent update date. Use the complete date as listed in the source. If a web source has no date, give your date of access at the end of the entry (*Accessed 24 Feb. 2021*). →

General guidelines for the works cited list (*cont.*)

Dates

- Abbreviate all months except May, June, and July and give the date in inverted form: *13 Mar. 2021*. September uses a four-character abbreviation: *Sept.*

Page numbers

- For most articles and other short works, give a page number when it is available in the source, preceded by *p.* (or *pp.* for more than one page).
- Do not use the page numbers from a printout of a source.
- If an article appears on nonconsecutive pages, give the number of the first page followed by a plus sign: *35+*.

URLs and DOIs

- Give a DOI (digital object identifier) if a source has one. Include the protocol and host (*https://doi.org/*). (See item 11.)
- If a source does not have a DOI, include a permalink if possible. Copy the permalink provided by the website.
- If a source does not have a permalink or a DOI, include a URL. Copy the URL directly from your browser. You may remove the protocol (*http://* or *https://*) if you do not need to provide live links for your readers. See also pages 32–33.
- If a URL is longer than three lines in the list of works cited, you may shorten it, leaving at least the website host (for example, *cnn.com* or *www.usda.gov*) in the entry.

General guidelines for listing authors

Alphabetize entries in the list of works cited by authors' last names (or by title if a work has no author). The author's name is important because citations in the text refer to it and readers will therefore look for the name to identify the source in the list of works cited.

1. Single author   Give the author's last name, followed by a comma, and then the first name and any middle initals, followed by a period.

Cronin, David.

2. Two authors List the authors in the order in which the source lists them. Reverse the name of only the first author.

Stiglitz, Joseph E., and Bruce C. Greenwald.

3. Three or more authors List the author whose name appears first in the source followed by *et al.* (Latin for "and others").

Lupton, Ellen, et al.

4. Organization or group author When the author is a corporation, an organization, or some other group, start the entry with the name of the group. Omit an article (*A, An,* or *The*) that begins the name. (For a source with a government agency listed as the author, see item 57.)

Coca-Cola Company.

Human Rights Watch.

Jackson 5.

5. Unknown author Begin with the work's title. In general, titles of short works are put in quotation marks and titles of long works are italicized.

ARTICLE OR OTHER SHORT WORK

"California Sues EPA over Emissions."

BOOK, ENTIRE WEBSITE, OR OTHER LONG WORK

Women of Protest: Photographs from the Records of the National Woman's Party.

6. Author using a pseudonym (pen name) Use the author's name as it appears in the source, followed by the author's real name in brackets, if you know it. Alternatively, if the author's real name is better known, you may start with that name, followed by *published as* and the pen name in brackets.

Saunders, Richard [Benjamin Franklin].

Franklin, Benjamin [*published as* Richard Saunders].

7. Screen name or social media account   Start with the account display name, followed by the screen name or handle (if available) in brackets. If the account name is a first and last name, invert it.

Gay, Roxane [@rgay].

Pat and Stewart [@grammarphobia].

If the account name and handle are very similar (for example, ACLU SoCal and @ACLU_SoCal), you may omit the handle. See items 39 and 40 for more on citing social media.

8. Multiple works by the same author   Alphabetize the works by title, ignoring (but not omitting) the article *A*, *An*, or *The* at the beginning. Use the author's name for the first entry only. For subsequent entries, use three hyphens or dashes followed by a period. Use three hyphens or dashes even when the author is a government agency or an organization.

Coates, Ta-Nehisi. *Between the World and Me.* Spiegel and Grau, 2015.

---. *We Were Eight Years in Power: An American Tragedy.* One World, 2018.

9. Multiple works by the same group of authors   When you cite multiple sources with the same group of authors (same lead author and coauthors), alphabetize the works by title. For the first entry, use the authors' names in the proper form (see items 1–4). Begin subsequent entries with three hyphens (or dashes) and a period.

Eaton-Robb, Pat, and Susan Haigh. "Pandemic May Lead to Long-Term Changes in School Calendar." *AP News,* 15 Apr. 2021, apnews.com/article/pandemics-connecticut-ned-lamont-975d41076ae6b9850 30c133614685f33.

---. "Rock Star Van Zandt Helping Connecticut Students Re-engage." *AP News,* 20 Apr. 2021, apnews.com/article/health-music-education-arts-and -entertainment-entertainment-5b038c218b30863d76031134db46fa5d.

Articles and other short works

10. Article in a magazine   Use the complete date given in the source. Give the volume number and issue number when available.

Owusu, Nadia. "Head Wraps." *The New York Times Magazine*, 7 Mar. 2021, p. 20.

Misner, Rebecca. "How I Became a Joiner." *Condé Nast Traveler*, vol. 5, 2018, pp. 55–56.

Stuart, Tessa. "New Study Suggests Burning Fossil Fuels Contributed to 1 in 5 Deaths in 2018." *Rolling Stone*, 17 Feb. 2021, www.rollingstone.com/politics/ politics-news/fossil-fuels-air-pollution-premature-deaths-statistics-1127586/.

Guerrero, Desirée. "All Genders, Period." *The Advocate*, no. 1105, Oct.–Nov. 2019, p. 31. *ProQuest*, www-proquest-com.proxy3.noblenet.org/ docview/2488268993.

11. Article in a journal   Give the volume number and issue number, if available, for all journals.

Matchie, Thomas. "Law versus Love in *The Round House*." *Midwest Quarterly*, vol. 56, no. 4, summer 2015, pp. 353–64.

Bryson, Devin. "The Rise of a New Senegalese Cultural Philosophy?" *African Studies Quarterly*, vol. 14, no. 3, Mar. 2014, pp. 33–56, asq.africa.ufl.edu/files/ Volume-14-Issue-3-Bryson.pdf.

Harris, Ashleigh May, and Nicklas Hållén. "African Street Literature: A Method for an Emergent Form beyond World Literature." *Research in African Literatures*, vol. 51, no. 2, summer 2020, pp. 1–26. *JSTOR*, https://doi.org/10.2979/ reseafrilite.51.2.01.

12. Article in a daily newspaper

Corasaniti, Nick, and Jim Rutenberg. "Record Turnout Hints at Future of Vote in U.S." *The New York Times*, 6 Dec. 2020, pp. A1+.

Jones, Ayana. "Chamber of Commerce Program to Boost Black-Owned Businesses." *The Philadelphia Tribune*, 21 Apr. 2021, www.phillytrib.com/news/business/ chamber-of-commerce-program-to-boost-black-owned-businesses/ article_6b14ae2f-5db2-5a59-8a67-8bbf974da451.html.

13. Editorial or op-ed   Add the word "Editorial" or "Op-ed" to the end of the entry if it is not clear from the author or title of the source.

Kansas City Star Editorial Board. "Kansas Considers Lowering Concealed Carry Age to 18. Why It's Wrong for Many Reasons." *The Kansas City Star*, 9 Mar. 2021, www.kansascity.com/opinion/editorials/article249793143.html.

Shribman, David M. "Gorman, Summoned to Participate, Is Celebrated." *Pittsburgh Post-Gazette*, 24 Jan. 2021, www.post-gazette.com/opinion/david -shribman/2021/01/24/Gorman-summoned-to-participate-is-celebrated/ stories/202101240042. Op-ed.

14. Letter to the editor   If the letter has no title or headline, use *Letter* in place of the title.

Rushlow, Lee. "My Recent Postal Ballot Was the Best I've Ever Cast." *The Wall Street Journal*, Dow Jones, 8 Oct. 2020, www.wsj.com/articles/my-recent -postal-ballot-was-the-best-ive-ever-cast-11602183549?reflink =desktopwebshare_permalink.

Carasso, Roger. Letter. *The New York Times*, 4 Apr. 2021, Sunday Book Review sec., p. 5.

15. Review   If the review is untitled, use the label *Review of* and the title and author or director of the work reviewed. Then add information for the publication in which the review appears.

Jopanda, Wayne Silao. Review of *America Is Not the Heart*, by Elaine Castillo. *Alon: Journal for Filipinx American and Diasporic Studies*, vol. 1, no. 1, Mar. 2021, pp. 106–08. *eScholarship*, escholarship.org/uc/item/0d44t8wx.

Bramesco, Charles. "*Honeyland* Couches an Apocalyptic Warning in a Beekeeping Documentary." *The A.V. Club*, G/O Media, 23 July 2019, film.avclub.com/ honeyland-couches-an-apocalyptic-warning-in-a-beekeepin-1836624795.

Books and other long works

16. Basic format for a book   For most books, supply the author name(s); the title and subtitle, in italics; the name of the publisher;

and the year of publication. If you have used an e-book, include "E-book ed." before the publisher name.

Cabral, Amber. *Allies and Advocates: Creating an Inclusive and Equitable Culture.* Wiley, 2021.

Cabral, Amber. *Allies and Advocates: Creating an Inclusive and Equitable Culture.* E-book ed., Wiley, 2021.

17. Audiobook   Give the author name and the title, each followed by a period. After the title, include the phrase *Narrated by* followed by the narrator's full name. If the author and narrator are the same, include only the last name. Then include "audiobook ed.," the publisher, and the year of release.

de Hart, Jane Sherron. *Ruth Bader Ginsburg: A Life.* Narrated by Suzanne Toren, audiobook ed., Random House Audio, 2018.

18. Author with an editor or a translator

Ullmann, Regina. *The Country Road: Stories.* Translated by Kurt Beals, New Directions Publishing, 2015.

19. Editor

Coates, Colin M., and Graeme Wynn, editors. *The Nature of Canada.* On Point Press, 2019.

20. Work in an anthology or a collection   Begin with the name of the author of the selection, not with the name of the anthology editor.

Symanovich, Alaina. "Compatibility." *Ab Terra 2020: A Science Fiction Anthology,* edited by Yen Ooi, Brain Mill Press, 2020, pp. 116–23.

21. Multiple works from the same anthology or collection   Provide an entry for the entire anthology and a shortened entry for each selection. Alphabetize the entries by authors' or editors' last names.

Challinor, Nels. "Porch Light." Ooi, pp. 107–15.

Ooi, Yen, editor. *Ab Terra 2020: A Science Fiction Anthology.* Brain Mill Press, 2020.

Symanovich, Alaina. "Compatibility." Ooi, pp. 116–23.

22. Edition other than the first

Walker, John A. *Art in the Age of Mass Media*. 3rd ed., Pluto Press, 2001.

23. Multivolume work Include the total number of volumes at the end of the citation. If the volumes were published over several years, give the inclusive dates of publication. If you cite only one of the volumes, include the volume number before the publisher and give the date of publication for that volume.

Brunetti, Ivan, editor. *An Anthology of Graphic Fiction, Cartoons, and True Stories*. Yale UP, 2006–08. 2 vols.

Brunetti, Ivan, editor. *An Anthology of Graphic Fiction, Cartoons, and True Stories*. Vol. 2, Yale UP, 2008.

If you cite one volume that is individually titled, include both the title of the volume and the title of the complete set.

Cather, Willa. *Willa Cather: Later Novels*. Edited by Sharon O'Brien, Library of America, 1990. Vol. 2 of *Willa Cather: The Complete Fiction and Other Writings*.

24. Encyclopedia or dictionary entry For an online source that is continually updated, such as a wiki entry, use the most recent update date.

Robinson, Lisa Clayton. "Harlem Writers Guild." *Africana: The Encyclopedia of the African and African American Experience*, edited by Kwame Anthony Appiah and Henry Louis Gates Jr., 2nd ed., Oxford UP, 2005, p. 163.

"House Music." *Wikipedia: The Free Encyclopedia*, Wikimedia Foundation, 8 Apr. 2021, en.wikipedia.org/wiki/House_music.

"Oligarchy, N." *Merriam-Webster*, 2021, www.merriam-webster.com/dictionary/oligarchy.

25. Sacred text Give the title of the edition of the sacred text (taken from the title page), italicized; the editor's or translator's name (if any); and publication information. Add the name of the version, if there is one, before the publisher.

Quran: The Final Testament. Translated by Rashad Khalifa, Authorized English Version with Arabic Text, Universal Unity, 2000.

The Oxford Annotated Bible with the Apocrypha. Edited by Herbert G. May and Bruce
M. Metzger, Revised Standard Version, Oxford UP, 1965.

26. Foreword, introduction, preface, or afterword   Begin with the
author of the book part, the part title (if any), and a label for the
part. Then give the title of the book, the author or editor preceded
by *by* or *edited by*, and publication information. If the part author
and book author are the same, use only the last name with the
book title.

Coates, Ta-Nehisi. Foreword. *The Origin of Others,* by Toni Morrison, Harvard UP,
2017, pp. vii–xvii.

27. Book with a title in its title   If the book title contains a title normally italicized, do not italicize the title within the book title. If
the book title contains a title normally placed in quotation marks,
retain the quotation marks and italicize the entire title.

Masur, Louis P. *Runaway Dream:* Born to Run *and Bruce Springsteen's American
Vision.* Bloomsbury Press, 2009.

Lethem, Jonathan. *"Lucky Alan" and Other Stories.* Doubleday, 2015.

28. Book in a series   After the publication information, list the
series name and the book's number in the series (if available) as it
appears on the title page.

Denham, A. E., editor. *Plato on Art and Beauty.* Palgrave Macmillan, 2012.
Philosophers in Depth.

29. Republished book   After the title of the book, cite the original
publication date, followed by the current publication information.

de Mille, Agnes. *Dance to the Piper.* 1951. New York Review Books, 2015.

30. More than one publisher named   If the book was published by
two or more publishers, separate the publishers with a slash, and
include a space before and after the slash.

Acevedo, Elizabeth. *With the Fire on High.* HarperTeen / Quill Tree Books, 2019.

31. Graphic narrative or illustrated work   If the author and illustrator are the same, cite the work as you would a book with one author (see items 1 and 16). When the author and illustrator are different, begin with the contributor who is most important to your research. List other contributors after the title, labeling their contribution. If there are multiple contributors but you are not discussing a specific contributor's work in your essay, you may begin with the title.

Martínez, Hugo, illustrator. *Wake: The Hidden History of Women-Led Slave Revolts.* By Rebecca Hall, Simon and Schuster, 2021.

Stealth. By Mike Costa, illustrated by Nate Bellegarde, colored by Tamra Bonvillain, lettered by Sal Cipriano, vol. 1, Image Comics, 2020.

32. Book in a language other than English   Capitalize the title according to the conventions of the book's language. Include an English translation of the title, in brackets, if your readers are not familiar with the book's language.

Vargas Llosa, Mario. *El sueño del celta [The Dream of the Celt].* Alfaguara Ediciones, 2010.

Online sources

33. Entire website   If the website does not have an update date, copyright date, or publication date, include your date of access at the end (see the second example in item 34.)

Lift Every Voice. Library of America / Schomburg Center for Research in Black Culture, 2020, africanamericanpoetry.org/.

34. Short work from a website

Enzinna, Wes. "Syria's Unknown Revolution." *Pulitzer Center,* 24 Nov. 2015, pulitzercenter.org/projects/middle-east-syria-enzinna-war-rojava.

Bali, Karan. "Shashikala." *Upperstall,* upperstall.com/profile/shashikala. Accessed 22 Apr. 2021.

35. Online book   After the book publication information, include the title of the site in italics and the URL for the work. If the book's original publication date is not available, include the date of online publication.

Euripides. *The Trojan Women*. Translated by Gilbert Murray, Oxford UP, 1915.
   Internet Sacred Text Archive, www.sacred-texts.com/cla/eurip/trojan.htm.

36. Entire blog   Cite a blog as you would an entire website (see item 33).

Ng, Amy. *Pikaland*. 2020, www.pikaland.com.

Horgan, John. *Cross-Check*. Scientific American, 2020, blogs.scientificamerican
   .com/cross-check/.

37. Blog post   Cite a blog post as you would a short work from a website (see item 34).

Horgan, John. "My Quantum Experiment." *Cross-Check*, Scientific American, 5 June
   2020, blogs.scientificamerican.com/cross-check/my-quantum-experiment/.

Edroso, Roy. "No Compassion." *Alicublog*, 18 Mar. 2021,
   alicublog.blogspot.com/2021/03/no-compassion.html.

38. Comment on a blog post or an online article   List the screen name of the commenter and use the label *Comment on* before the title of the post or article. Include the URL to the comment when possible; otherwise, use the URL for the post or article.

satch. Comment on "No Compassion," by Roy Edroso. *Alicublog*, 20 Mar. 2021,
   9:50 a.m., disq.us/p/2fuOulk.

39. Tweet   Give either the text of the entire tweet in quotation marks, using the writer's capitalization and punctuation, or a brief description if you are focusing on a visual element of the tweet rather than the text in your work. Follow with *Twitter*, then provide the date and end with the URL. (See item 7 for how to style screen names.)

Abdurraqib, Hanif [@NifMuhammad]. "Tracy Chapman really one of the greatest Ohio writers." *Twitter*, 30 Mar. 2021, twitter.com/NifMuhammad/ status/1377086355667320836.

40. Other posts on social media   Cite as a short work from a website (see item 34). If the post does not have a title, use the text accompanying the post, if it is brief, as the title; if the post is long, use the first few words followed by an ellipsis. If the post has no title or text, or if you are focusing on a visual element rather than the text in your work, provide a description of the post. (See item 7 for how to style screen names.)

ACLU. "Public officials have . . . ." *Facebook*, 10 May 2021, www.facebook.com/ aclu/photos/a.74134381812/10157852911711813.

Rosa, Camila [camixvx]. Illustration of nurses in masks with fists raised. *Instagram*, 28 Apr. 2020, www.instagram.com/p/B_h62W9pJaQ/.

Jones, James [@notoriouscree]. "Some traditional hoop teachings #indigenous #culture #native #powwow." *TikTok*, 6 Apr. 2021, www.tiktok.com/ @notoriouscree/video/6948207430610226438.

Visual, audio, multimedia, and live sources

41. Work of art or photograph   Cite the artist's name; the title of the artwork or photograph, italicized; and the date of composition. For works viewed in person, include the institution and the city in which the artwork is located after the date and a comma. For works located online, include the title of the site and the URL of the work after the date and a period.

Bronzino, Agnolo. *Lodovico Capponi*. 1550–55, Frick Collection, New York.

Lange, Dorothea. *Migrant Mother, Nipomo, California*. Mar. 1936. *MOMA*, www.moma.org/collection/works/50989.

42. Cartoon or comic strip

Shiell, Mike. Cartoon. *The Saturday Evening Post*, Jan.–Feb. 2021, p. 8.

Munroe, Randall. "Heartbleed Explanation." *xkcd*, xkcd.com/1354/. Accessed 10
Oct. 2020.

43. Advertisement

Advertisement for Better World Club. *Mother Jones*, Mar.–Apr. 2021, p. 2.

"The Whole Working-from-Home Thing — Apple." *YouTube*, uploaded by Apple, 13
July 2020, www.youtube.com/watch?v=6_pru8U2RmM.

44. Map or chart   If the map or chart is located in another source,
cite it as a short work within a longer work. If the title does not
identify the item as a map or chart, add *Map* or *Chart* at the end
of the entry.

"Australia." *Perry-Castañeda Library Map Collection*, U of Texas Libraries, 2016,
legacy.lib.utexas.edu/maps/cia16/australia_sm_2016.gif.

"New COVID-19 Cases Worldwide." *Coronavirus Resource Center*, Johns Hopkins U
and Medicine, 3 May 2021, coronavirus.jhu.edu/data/new-cases. Chart.

45. Musical score

Beethoven, Ludwig van. *Symphony No. 5 in C Minor, Opus 67*. 1807. Center for
Computer Assisted Research in the Humanities, 2008, scores.ccarh.org/
beethoven/sym/beethoven-sym5-1.pdf.

46. Music recording   Begin with the name of the person or group
you want to emphasize. For a single work from an album or collection, place the title in quotation marks and the album or collection in italics. For a long work, give the title, italicized. Provide
the names of relevant artists and the orchestra and conductor (if
any), the record label, and the date. If you listen to the recording
online, include the URL for the recording or the name of the app.

Bach, Johann Sebastian. *Bach: Violin Concertos*. Performances by Itzhak Perlman,
Pinchas Zukerman, and English Chamber Orchestra, EMI, 2002.

Bad Bunny. "Vete." *YHLQMDLG*, Rimas, 2020. *Apple Music* app.

47. Film or movie   If you focus on a particular person's work, start
with that name. If not, start with the title of the film; then give the

director, distributor or production company, and year of release. Other contributors, such as writers or performers, may follow the director. If you viewed the film on a streaming service, include the app or the website name and URL at the end of the entry. See item 53 for how to cite online videos (from *YouTube* or *Vimeo*, for example).

Judas and the Black Messiah. Directed by Shaka King, Warner Bros. Pictures, 2021.

Youn, Yuh-Jung, performer. *Minari*. Directed by Lee Isaac Chung, Plan B Entertainment / A24, 2020. *Amazon Prime Video* app.

Kubrick, Stanley, director. *A Clockwork Orange*. Hawk Films / Warner Bros. Pictures, 1971. *Netflix*, www.netflix.com.

48. Supplementary material accompanying a film   Begin with the title of the feature, in quotation marks, and the names of any important contributors. End with information about the film, as in item 47, and about the location of the supplementary material.

"Sweeney's London." Produced by Eric Young. *Sweeney Todd: The Demon Barber of Fleet Street*, directed by Tim Burton, DreamWorks Pictures, 2007, disc 2. DVD.

49. Radio or television program   If you are citing a particular episode or segment, begin with the title in quotation marks. Then give the program title in italics. List important contributors (creator, writer, director, narrator, actors), if relevant to your writing; the season and episode numbers; the network, distributor, or production company; and the date of broadcast or publication. Unless you viewed or listened to the program on a live broadcast, end with the site or service on which you accessed it.

"Umbrellas Down." *This American Life*, hosted by Ira Glass, WBEZ, 10 July 2020.

"Shock and Delight." *Bridgerton*, season 1, episode 2, Shondaland / Netflix, 2020. *Netflix*, www.netflix.com.

Hillary. Directed by Nanette Burstein, Propagate Content / Hulu, 2020. *Hulu* app.

If there is an episode-specific contributor, you may include that person's name after the episode title.

50. Radio or television interview Begin with the name of the person who was interviewed, followed by *Interview by* and the interviewer's name, if relevant. End with information about the program as in item 49.

Kendi, Ibram X. Interview by Eric Deggans. *Life Kit*, NPR, 24 Oct. 2020.

51. Podcast series or episode Cite as you would a television series or episode (see item 49).

"Childish Gambino: *Because the Internet.*" *Dissect*, hosted by Cole Cuchna, season 7, episode 1, Spotify, Sep. 2020. *Spotify* app.

Dolly Parton's America. Hosted by Jad Abumrad, produced and reported by Shima Oliaee, WNYC Studios, 2019, www.wnycstudios.org/podcasts/dolly-partons-america.

52. Stand-alone audio segment

"The Past Returns to Gdańsk." Written and narrated by Michael Segalov, *BBC*, 26 Apr. 2021, www.bbc.co.uk/sounds/play/m000vh4f.

53. Online video If the video is viewed on a video-sharing site such as *YouTube* or *Vimeo*, put the name of the uploader after the name of the website. If the video emphasizes a single speaker or presenter, as some TED Talks do, list that person as the author.

"The Art of Single Stroke Painting in Japan." *YouTube*, uploaded by National Geographic, 13 July 2018, www.youtube.com/watch?v=g7H8IhGZnpM.

Kundu, Anindya. "The 'Opportunity Gap' in US Public Education — and How to Close It." *TED*, May 2019, www.ted.com/talks/anindya_kundu_the_opportunity _gap_in_us_public_education_and_how_to_close_it.

54. Live performance Begin with either the title of the work performed or, if relevant, the author, composer, or main performer. After the title, include relevant contributors (director, choreographer, conductor, major performers). End with the theater, ballet, or opera company, if any; the date of the performance; and the location.

Beethoven, Ludwig van. *Piano Concerto No. 3*. Conducted by Andris Nelsons, performed by Paul Lewis and Boston Symphony Orchestra, 9 Oct. 2015, Symphony Hall, Boston.

Schreck, Heidi. *What the Constitution Means to Me*. Directed by Oliver Butler, 16 June 2019, Helen Hayes Theater, New York City.

55. Lecture or public address   Cite the speaker's name, followed by the title of the lecture (if any) in quotation marks; the organization sponsoring the lecture; the date; and the location. If the lecture or address has no title, use the label "Lecture" or "Address" after the speaker's name.

Gay, Roxane. "Difficult Women, Bad Feminists and Unruly Bodies." Beatty Lecture Series, 18 Oct. 2018, McGill University.

56. Personal interview   Begin with the name of the person interviewed. Then describe the type of interview, followed by the date of the interview.

Freedman, Sasha. Video interview with the author. 10 Nov. 2020.

Other sources

57. Government publication   Give the name of the author as presented by the source.

U.S. Bureau of Labor Statistics. "Consumer Expenditures Report 2019." *BLS Reports*, Dec. 2020, www.bls.gov/opub/reports/consumer-expenditures/2019/home.htm.

If you use several government sources, you may want to standardize your list of works cited by listing the name of the government, spelled out, followed by the name of any agencies and subagencies.

United States, Department of Labor, Bureau of Labor Statistics. "Consumer Expenditures Report 2019." *BLS Reports*, Dec. 2020, www.bls.gov/opub/reports/consumer-expenditures/2019/home.htm.

58. Legal source   For a legislative act (law), give the government body, the Public Law number, and the publication information.

United States, Congress. Public Law 116-136. *United States Statutes at Large*, vol. 134, 2019, pp. 281–615. *U.S. Government Publishing Office*, www.govinfo .gov/content/pkg/PLAW-116publ136/uslm/PLAW-116publ136.xml.

For a court case, name the court and then name the case. Give the date of the decision and the publication information.

United States, Supreme Court. *Miller v. Alabama*. 25 June 2012. *Legal Information Institute*, Cornell Law School, www.law.cornell.edu/supremecourt/
   . text/10-9646.

59. Pamphlet or brochure

Sierra County Public Health. *Benefits of the COVID-19 Vaccine*. 2021, sierracounty .ca.gov/DocumentCenter/View/5522/Benefits-of-the-COVID-19-Vaccine -Brochure. Brochure.

60. Dissertation

Kabugi, Magana J. *The Souls of Black Colleges: Cultural Production, Ideology, and Identity at Historically Black Colleges and Universities*. 2020. Vanderbilt U, PhD dissertation. *Vanderbilt University Institutional Repository*, hdl.handle .net/1803/16103.

61. Published proceedings of a conference

Zhang, Baosheng, et al., editors. *A Dialogue between Law and History: Proceedings of the Second International Conference on Facts and Evidence*. Springer, 2021.

62. Published interview   (See item 56 for a personal interview.)

Harjo, Joy. "The First Native American U.S. Poet Laureate on How Poetry Can Counter Hate." Interview by Olivia B. Waxman. *Time*, 22 Aug. 2019, time .com/5658443/joy-harjo-poet-interview/.

63. Personal communication

Primak, Shoshana. Text message to the author. 6 May 2021.

Lewis-Truth, Antoine. E-mail to the Office of Student Financial Assistance. 30 Aug. 2020.

64. Classroom materials   For materials posted to an online learning management system, include as much information as is available about the source (author, title or description, and any publication information); then give the course, instructor, platform, institution name, date of posting, and URL. For materials delivered in a print or PDF course pack, include the author and title of the work; the words "Course pack for" with the course number and name; "compiled by" with the instructor's name; the term; and the institution name.

Rose, Mike. "Blue-Collar Brilliance." Introduction to College Writing, taught by
    Melanie Li. *Blackboard,* Merrimack College, 9 Sept. 2020, blackboard
    .merrimack.edu/ultra/courses/_25745_1/cl/readings.

MLA-style formatting

The following guidelines are consistent with advice given in the *MLA Handbook,* 9th edition (2021), and with typical requirements for student projects. If you are creating a nonprint project or have formatting questions, it's always a good idea to check with your instructor before preparing your final draft.

Formatting an MLA project

Margins and spacing.   Leave one-inch margins at the top and bottom and on both sides of each page. Double-space the entire text, including set-off quotations, notes, tables, and the list of works cited. Indent the first line of a paragraph one-half inch.

First page and title page.   For a project authored by an individual writer, a title page is not needed. Type each of the following items on a separate double-spaced line on the first page of your essay, beginning one inch from the top and aligned with the left margin: your name, the instructor's name, the course name and number, and the date. On the next line, place the title, centered, with no additional spacing above or below the title. See page 34 for an example.

For a group project, create a title page with all members' names, the instructor's name, the course, and the date, all left-aligned on separate double-spaced lines. Center the title on a new line a few spaces down. See page 41 for an example.

Page numbers. Include your last name and the page number on each page, one-half inch below the top of the page and aligned with the right margin. For a group project, include all members' last names and the page number; if the names will not all fit on a single line, include only the page number on each page.

Long quotations. Set off a long quotation (one with more than four typed lines) in block format by starting it on a new line and indenting each line one-half inch from the left margin. Do not enclose the passage in quotation marks. See page 37 for an example.

Headings. While headings are generally not needed for brief essays, readers may find them helpful for long or complex essays. Place each heading in the same style and size. If you need subheadings (level 2, level 3), be consistent in styling them. Place headings at the left margin without any indent. Capitalize headings as you would titles. See page 39 for an example.

Visuals. Place tables, photographs, drawings, charts, graphs, and other visuals as near as possible to the relevant text. A table should have a label and number (*Table 1*) and a clear title, each on its own line above the table and aligned with the left margin. For a table that you have borrowed or adapted, give the source below the table in a note like the following:

Source: Boris Groysberg and Michael Slind. "Leadership Is a Conversation." *Harvard Business Review*, June 2012, p. 83.

All other visuals should be labeled *Figure* (usually abbreviated *Fig.*), numbered, and captioned below the visual. The label and caption should appear on the same line. If your caption includes full source information and you do not cite the source anywhere else in your text, it is not necessary to include an entry in your list of works cited. Remember to refer to each visual in your text, indicating how it contributes to the point you are making: *see table 1; as shown in figure 2.*

See pages 35 and 36 for examples of a table and a visual.

Formatting an MLA works cited list

Begin the list of works cited on a new page at the end of the project. Center the title *Works Cited* one inch from the top of the page. Double-space throughout.

Alphabetizing the list. Alphabetize the list by the last names of the authors (or the names of corporate or government authors); if a work has no author, alphabetize by the first word of the title other than *A, An,* or *The.*

Indenting the entries. Do not indent the first line of each works cited entry, but indent any additional lines one-half inch. This is called a *hanging indent.*

Including URLs. If you include a URL in a works cited entry, copy the URL directly from your browser. If the entire URL moves to another line, creating a short line, you may leave it that way. Do not add any hyphens or spaces.

Kundu, Anindya. "The 'Opportunity Gap' in US Public Education — and How to Close It." *TED*, May 2019,
https://www.ted.com/talks/anindya_kundu_the_opportunity_gap_in_us_
public_education_and_how_to_close_it.

Professionally typeset works, such as this booklet, may introduce line breaks to avoid uneven line displays.

If a URL is longer than three lines in the list of works cited, you may shorten it, leaving at least the website host (for example, *cnn.com* or *www.usda.gov*) in the entry. If you will post your project online or submit it electronically and you want your readers to click on your URLs, do not insert any line breaks, shorten the URL, or delete the protocol (*https://* or *http://*).

Sample pages from student writing in MLA style

The following pages feature examples from a variety of student essays. The sample pages show the writers following MLA guidelines for formatting a basic essay (p. 34), placing and labeling visuals (pp. 35–36), formatting long quotations (p. 37), styling headings (p. 39), composing a list of works cited (p. 40), creating a title page for a group project (p. 41), and citing sources (throughout).

Basic format; first text page

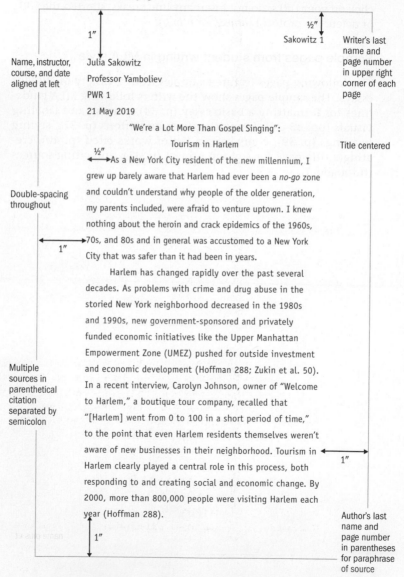

Name, instructor, course, and date aligned at left

1″

Julia Sakowitz

Professor Yamboliev

PWR 1

21 May 2019

½″ Sakowitz 1

Writer's last name and page number in upper right corner of each page

"We're a Lot More Than Gospel Singing":

Tourism in Harlem

Title centered

½″
As a New York City resident of the new millennium, I grew up barely aware that Harlem had ever been a *no-go* zone and couldn't understand why people of the older generation, my parents included, were afraid to venture uptown. I knew nothing about the heroin and crack epidemics of the 1960s, 70s, and 80s and in general was accustomed to a New York City that was safer than it had been in years.

Double-spacing throughout

1″

Harlem has changed rapidly over the past several decades. As problems with crime and drug abuse in the storied New York neighborhood decreased in the 1980s and 1990s, new government-sponsored and privately funded economic initiatives like the Upper Manhattan Empowerment Zone (UMEZ) pushed for outside investment and economic development (Hoffman 288; Zukin et al. 50). In a recent interview, Carolyn Johnson, owner of "Welcome to Harlem," a boutique tour company, recalled that "[Harlem] went from 0 to 100 in a short period of time," to the point that even Harlem residents themselves weren't aware of new businesses in their neighborhood. Tourism in Harlem clearly played a central role in this process, both responding to and creating social and economic change. By 2000, more than 800,000 people were visiting Harlem each year (Hoffman 288).

Multiple sources in parenthetical citation separated by semicolon

1″

1″

Author's last name and page number in parentheses for paraphrase of source

Table in text

Wang 4

Table 1

Comparison of Two Approaches to Teaching and Learning

Teaching and Learning Period	Instructor-Centered Approach	Student-Centered Approach
Before Class	• Instructor prepares lesson on new topic. • Students do HW on previous topic.	• Students read new material, prepare questions. • Instructor views student work.
During Class	• Instructor delivers new lesson. • Students— unprepared— try to follow along with new material.	• Students lead discussions of new material in active environment. • Instructor provides feedback.
After Class	• Instructor grades HW from previous lesson. • Students work alone to practice concepts.	• Students apply concepts alone and in groups. • Instructor posts resources for help.

Adapted from: "The Flipped Class Demystified." *NYU,* www.nyu .edu/faculty/teaching-and-learning-resources/strategies -for-teaching-with-tech/flipped-classes/the-flipped-class -demystified.html. Accessed 6 Mar. 2018.

    A Stanford study came to a similar conclusion; researchers examined four schools that had moved from teacher-driven instruction to student-centered learning (Friedlaender et al.). The study focused on students from

---

Table number and title given on separate lines above table

Double-spacing throughout

Source information provided in caption

First author's name plus *et al.* for source with three or more authors

Visual in text

Bryan 4

Shortened title used for source with no author; full title is "Voter ID 101: The Right to Vote Shouldn't Come with Barriers"

elderly, people of color, and people with low incomes" ("Voter ID"). If the United States wants to empower all people's voices, then there should be as few barriers to the voting process as possible. Many continue to advocate for voter ID laws, citing how easily its abolition could lead to voter fraud. However, this notion has already been disputed: one study found only thirty-one credible incidents of voter impersonation out of more than one billion ballots cast between 2000 to 2014, whereas in only four states during this same time period "more than 3,000 votes (in general elections alone) have reportedly been affirmatively rejected

Only author name appears in parentheses for unpaginated online source

for lack of ID" (Levitt). Studies like these highlight both the uselessness and the harm of voter ID laws.

In addition to voter ID laws, some voters are held up by prohibitively long lines, seen in figure 1, and mishandling of polling procedures. The Democratic Party of Georgia even

Reference to figure in text

ETHAN MILLER/GETTY IMAGES

Figure number and caption providing source information

Fig. 1. Ethan Miller. *Five States Hold Primaries as Pandemic Continues in America*. 9 June 2020. *Getty Images*, www .gettyimages.com/detail/news-photo/people-who-are-registering -to-vote-or-who-need-a-ballot-news-photo/1248635497.

When full publication information is given in caption, no entry is needed in list of works cited

Internal text page, sample 1

Sakowitz 4

For example, Harlem is internationally famous as a "Black
Mecca," yet it is also more than half Latino and a center for
"Nuyorican" identity, urban Latindad, and Latino dance and
music (Dávila 52). But what happens when visitors' needs and
residents' reality just don't align? Dávila writes:

> By limiting East Harlem's funding eligibility to
> certain sections and imposing requirements that only
> institutionalized cultural industries could meet, EZ
> virtually guaranteed that cultural institutions in Central
> and West Harlem, which are the most established
> cultural institutions in Upper Manhattan, would be
> most prominently featured in EZ-sponsored tourist
> promotional materials and the ones eligible for the
> largest amounts of funding. (51)

When Latino cultural initiatives have applied for
UMEZ funding, the UMEZ board has questioned the appeal of
Latino culture, in one instance rejecting a salsa museum's
application because it doubted the international popularity
of salsa and the museum's ability to create at least five
jobs (Dávila 59). The results of such policy for El Barrio are
dramatic: Dávila estimates that as little as six percent of the
UMEZ cultural funding was given to Latino initiatives (51).

But Latino Harlemites aren't the only ones who suffer
from the UMEZ policies. Deborah Faison, a Harlem resident,
commented that the technical training the UMEZ provides is
"by itself . . . not enough" and that it's necessary to be "in
a strong position already to participate" in the program (qtd.
in Maurrasse 164). Carolyn Johnson, who receives funding for
"Welcome to Harlem" through the UMEZ, believes that UMEZ

Annotations:

Long quotation of more than four lines indented 1/2" from left margin

Signal phrase names author

Page number in parentheses after period

Indirect quotation uses *qtd. in* and last name of the author of the source in list of works cited

Internal text page, sample 2

Harba 4

Full author
name used in
signal phrase

No page
number for
unpaginated
online source

Citation for
source with two
authors uses
and

Ellipsis (three
spaced
periods) used
to indicate
words removed
from quotation

Shortened
name used in
parenthetical
citation instead of
long organization
name: *National
Center for
Chronic Disease
Prevention and
Health Promotion*

Michael Pollan, who has written extensively about
Americans' unhealthy eating habits, notes that "[t]he Centers for
Disease Control estimates that fully three quarters of US health
care spending goes to treat chronic diseases, most of which
are preventable and linked to diet: heart disease, stroke, type 2
diabetes, and at least a third of all cancers." In fact, the amount
of money the United States spends to treat chronic illnesses is
increasing so rapidly that the Centers for Disease Control has
labeled chronic disease "the public health challenge of the 21st
century" (National Center 1). In fighting this epidemic, the
primary challenge is not the need to find a cure; the challenge
is to prevent chronic diseases from striking in the first place.

Legislation, however, is not a popular solution when it
comes to most Americans and the food they eat. According to a
nationwide poll, seventy-five percent of Americans are opposed
to laws that restrict or put limitations on access to unhealthy
foods (Neergaard and Agiesta). When New York mayor Michael
Bloomberg proposed a regulation in 2012 banning the sale of
soft drinks in servings greater than twelve ounces in restaurants
and movie theaters, he was ridiculed as "Nanny Bloomberg."
In California in 2011, legislators failed to pass a law that
would impose a penny-per-ounce tax on soda, which would
have funded obesity prevention programs. And in Mississippi,
legislators passed "a ban on bans—a law that forbids . . . local
restrictions on food or drink" (Conly A23).

Why is the public largely resistant to laws that would
limit unhealthy choices or penalize those choices with
so-called fat taxes? Many consumers and civil rights advocates
find such laws to be an unreasonable restriction on individual

Internal text page, sample 3

Riew 4

over the world based on several criteria, including "excellent health and housing; positive social interactions . . . ; [and] safe and stimulating environments" (American Humane). Regulations are a step in the right direction.

Benefits of Regulations

With animal welfare regulations, zoos will protect animals at a higher standard than they have in the past—sometimes at a higher standard than animals can find in the wild if their habitat has been disrupted. Ron Kagan, CEO of the Detroit Zoological Society, points to the success of the Arctic Ring of Life, the largest polar bear facility in the United States. The facility provides chilled seawater and a safe environment for bears whose polar habitats have been destroyed by climate change (00:07:40–08:36). Kagan argues that by putting the needs of the animals first, regulated zoos create living environments that can be both safe and comfortable for animals, giving them access to shelter and space that they may no longer find in the wild.

To some critics, capturing and breeding endangered animals in such situations—when the animals may no longer be able to survive in their natural habitats—is pointless. These critics argue that breeding and captive protection can be permissible only if zoos eventually release the animals. However, research indicates that the majority of captive species fail to flourish once reintroduced into their natural habitats: one particularly devastating reintroduction study revealed that "only 16 out of 145 reintroduction projects using captive-born animals were successful" (Keulartz 341). Once in captivity, animals

Brackets indicate change to quotation; no page number for unpaginated source

Heading, aligned left, indicates new section in a longer essay

Time stamp provided for video source

Author's last name and page number in parentheses for quotation

Works cited list

Heading centered

Article from a database with DOI

Personal interview

Short work from a website

Source with no author begins with title

Source with three or more authors uses *et al.*

Sakowitz 10

Works Cited

Dávila, Arlene. "Empowered Culture? New York City's Empowerment Zone and the Selling of El Barrio." *The Annals of the American Academy of Political and Social Science*, vol. 594, no. 1, July 2004, pp. 49–64. *SAGE Journals,* https://doi.org/10.1177/0002716204264940.

Fainstein, Susan S., and John C. Powers. "Tourism and New York's Ethnic Diversity: An Underutilized Resource?" *Tourism, Ethnic Diversity and the City*, edited by Jan Rath, Routledge, 2007, pp. 143–63.

Johnson, Carolyn D. "About Us." *Welcome to Harlem*, welcometoharlem.com/page/about-us/. Accessed 15 May 2019.

---. Interview with the author. 9 May 2019.

Maurrasse, David J. *Listening to Harlem: Gentrification, Community, and Business*. Routledge, 2006.

Schulz, Dana. "House Tours Galore: Where to Get a Look inside the Area's Most Fabulous Homes and Gardens." *6sqft*, 5 May 2015, www.6sqft.com/house-tours-galore-where-to-get-a-look-inside-the-areas-most-fabulous-homes-and-gardens/.

"Upper Manhattan Empowerment Zone: Who We Are." *Upper Manhattan Empowerment Zone Development Corporation*, umez.org. Accessed 12 May 2019.

Zukin, Sharon, et al. "New Retail Capital and Neighborhood Change: Boutiques and Gentrification in New York City." *City & Community*, vol. 8, no. 1, Mar. 2009, pp. 47–64.

List of works cited starts on new page, but pagination is continuous

Source with two authors uses *and*

Second source by same author uses three hyphens instead of author name

Second and subsequent lines of each entry are indented

Access date provided for web page with no date

Title page for group project

Title page
created for
group project; all
authors' names,
instructor's name,
course title, and
date listed in a
heading aligned
left

Nikole Carter

Andrea Hidalgo-Vásquez

Jaylen Johnson

Sujan Kapoor

Professor Hamada

English 102

29 April 2021

Running head
starts on first text
page, not title
page; for group
project, all author
last names and
page number
appear in
running head; if
all names do not
fit, include only
page number

Title centered a
few lines down
from heading

Still Alice and Representations of Aging in America